101

Ideas For
Making Family Memories

Ruthann Winans and Linda Lee

Artwork by Lila Rose Kennedy

HARVEST HOUSE PUBLISHERS
EUGENE, OR

"Grandma's Snowball Cookies" (#14) are compliments of Linda's 90-year-old grandmother, Naomi Winans.

101 Ideas for Making Family Memories

Text Copyright © 2000 by Ruthann Winans and Linda Lee
Published by Harvest House Publishers
Eugene, Oregon 97402

ISBN 0-7369-0223-6

Artwork designs are reproduced under license from © Arts Uniq'®, Inc., Cookeville, TN and may not be reproduced without permission. For information regarding art prints featured in this book, please contact:

> Arts Uniq'
> P.O. Box 3085
> Cookeville, TN 38502
> 800-223-5020

Design and production by Garborg Design Works, Minneapolis, Minnesota

Scripture quotations are from the Holy Bible, New Living Translation, copyright © 1996. Used by permission of Tyndale House Publishers, Inc., Wheaton, Illinois 60189; and from the Holy Bible, New International Version®, Copyright 1973, 1978, 1984 by the International Bible Society. Used by permission of Zondervan Publishing House.

Printed in China.

00 01 02 03 04 05 06 07 08 09 /PP/ 10 9 8 7 6 5 4 3 2 1

Giving Love a Memory

We long to give our children special memories. We want them to look back fondly on celebrations and family moments, remembering them as happy and filled with love. But we sometimes lose our way; we fill our days so full we hardly have time to breathe.

The best gift you can give your children is *you!* So make a commitment to simplify your life as much as possible. Choose just a few creative, memorable things to try with your children, then relax and have fun while you do them. Sing, smile, laugh, hold hands, savor the moments you have together. You'll be creating the memories your family will treasure most.

1 Be a Secret Angel

Put everyone's name in a basket and after dinner have each person draw a name. For the next week, each person must try to do a good deed or leave special surprises in secret for the other. When the week is over, try to guess who has been your secret angel.

May the LORD reward you for your kindness.
THE BOOK OF RUTH

2 Old-Fashioned Carolers

You don't have to carol only at Christmastime! After dinner pile everyone in the car and go for a drive to a friend's or family member's house. On the way, practice a song or two to sing at their door.

3 Classic Movie Night

For something fun on a cold winter's night, rent some movie classics, get out your fluffiest blankets and your slippers, and snuggle up. During intermission make some indoor snowballs to eat.

INDOOR SNOWBALL: Quickly roll scoops of hard ice cream in mounds of shredded coconut. Serve snowball on a chilled platter with chocolate sauce, nuts, and sprinkles on the side.

4 Card Party

Homemade cards add your family's touch to special occasions like Christmas, Easter, and Valentine's Day. Turn card making into a party by having treats and drinks for all your hard workers. Have plenty of construction paper, wrapping paper, stickers, stamps, glitter, and so forth on hand. Encourage everyone to use their creativity and to put their name on the back of the cards they make (just like Hallmark!).

5 For the Birds

Decorate one of your outdoor trees with food for the birds. Frost pine cones or jar lids with peanut butter and tie them to the tree with colorful ribbons. Fill orange rinds with birdseed and nestle them among the boughs. Use a squeeze bottle to drizzle honey over branches. String popcorn or cranberries and drape on the tree. These are all treats your feathered friends will cherish!

6 A Very Merry Snowman

If you're fortunate enough to enjoy lots of that fluffy white stuff during the winter, remember to take the time to play! For a very merry snowman, fill several spray bottles with water and food coloring and give your snowman a colorful outfit to wear. Add just the right amount of winter blush to his smiling face.

7 Winter Picnic

Pack a breakfast or a lunch to have in the woods on a cold winter's day. Make your winter picnic complete by gathering the family around a cozy campfire where they can happily warm their frozen fingers and toes. Cook up a few tasty treats: Try hickory-smoked bacon and scrambled eggs for breakfast or grill hot dogs for a lunch that everyone will love. You can fill the frosty winter air with a cozy scent as you simmer spicy whole cloves and cinnamon sticks in a kettle of fresh apple cider. And no one can resist the chocolate goodness of a steaming cup of cocoa topped with marshmallows.

Teddy Bear Bread

Thaw store-bought frozen bread dough and divide it into teddy bear-size pieces. Make larger pieces for the head and tummy and smaller ones for the legs, ears, and nose. Assemble the pieces on a greased cookie sheet. Pinch together the doughy bear parts, adding raisin eyes and the nose. Cover the bear with a clean towel and allow it to rise for 1 hour. Paint an egg-white glaze over the entire bear. Bake the bear at 350° for 25 minutes or until golden brown. To give as a gift, tie a red ribbon around its neck.

9 Homemade Snowflakes

With a glue gun, put together Popsicle sticks or tongue depressors into a snowflake shape (create a plus sign [+] then add an "x"). Paint both sides of your snowflake white and add iridescent glitter while the paint is wet.

When dry, cut a slit on both sides of one stick, about one-half inch from the end, then tie clear fishing line around the slits to hang.

10 Your Very Own Snow Family

For a real show-stopper, create a snow family representing each member of your family! Have the members of your family share old stocking caps, mittens, even unused eyeglasses to create your own look-alike snowman. Don't forget to give your snowmen cheerful, rosy cheeks by spraying a combination of water and a few drops of red food coloring with a pump spray bottle.

11 Remember That Tune!

To add an element of joyful surprise and humor into your home, choose a lively tune to become your family's own. Every time you hear it played, stop what you are doing and join together for a family march throughout the rooms of your house, singing along at the top of your lungs!

12 Let's Draw a Birthday!

Make a list of birthday words that can be easily illustrated: candles, cake, party hat, ice cream, presents, and so on. Then cut the list into separate strips of paper and put the strips into a bowl. Everyone takes a turn pulling out a "birthday word" and tries to draw it in one minute or less (use kitchen timer), while the others try to guess what it is.

13 Thanks for the Memories

Make writing thank-you notes a treat rather than a chore. Put together a basket of thank-you cards, envelopes, postage stamps, colorful stickers, and an address book. Have your children help you pick out these items. When it's time to send a thank you, pull out your specially prepared basket.

14 Grandma's Snowball Cookies

When rolled in powdered sugar these special cookies really resemble miniature snowballs. It's a perfect treat with hot cocoa!

Ingredients: 1 C flour; 1/2 C butter; 2 T sugar; 1 C chopped nuts; 1/8 t salt; 1 t vanilla. Cream all ingredients together then mold into small balls. Place on a greased cookie sheet. Bake 15 minutes at 350°. Roll in powdered sugar.

15 Memories of Times Past

Send a blank cassette tape to relatives who live far away. Ask them to record some of their favorite memories. Include a postage-paid envelope to make it as convenient as possible for them to return the tape to you. When the tape arrives, plan an evening to listen to this special recording while eating a yummy dessert.

16 Hospitality Basket

During the holidays, keep a basket near your front door filled with wrapped goodies for your children to give to friends who stop by . . . and for those last-minute gifts you may need. You can fill this basket with homemade treats like hot cocoa mix, cookies and candies packaged in jars, little cellophane bags, or brown lunch sacks tied with a ribbon.

Practice hospitality.
THE BOOK OF ROMANS

17 Homemade Cocoa Mix

This is a simple, homemade gift children can easily make.
Ingredients: 3 C chocolate powdered drink mix; 2 C powdered sugar; 1 11-oz. jar powdered creamer; 10 C powdered milk; 1 bag miniature marshmallows.

Mix ingredients thoroughly in a large bowl. Pour the cocoa mix into jars. Decorate the jar lids with fabric and a raffia bow. Attach a card with these simple directions: "Add three heaping tablespoons to a cup of hot water. May it warm you from head to toe!"

18 A "Little House" Evening

Plan a "Little House on the Prairie" evening. Start by turning off the television, radio, and as many electric lights as possible. Light a fire or candles. See how many things you can do by candlelight. Can you read? Brush your teeth? Play checkers? Take a bath? Before bedtime, be sure to read from *Little House on the Prairie* by Laura Ingalls Wilder.

19 Snowman Pancakes

Pour a large, medium, and small scoop of batter close together on a hot griddle and let them connect together while they cook—forming a snowman. When finished cooking, sprinkle with a little powdered sugar and add chocolate chip eyes, nose, and buttons.

20 A No-Fuss Family Concert

First, decide on a name for your group (for example, the Montana Monotones or Harrison Harmonics). Have the children make concert posters using colored paper and crayons or marking pens to display around the house. Then help them make refreshments for the intermission. On the big night, gather in the living room. In age-order (youngest to oldest), each person stands and leads the "choir" in his or her favorite song.

21 Birthday Celebration Place Mats

Have each member of your family design a place mat that illustrates his or her favorite things about birthdays. Simply cut place mats out of poster board and decorate them using wrapping paper, magazines, markers, fancy-edged scissors, craft supplies, family photos, stories, and sayings. Sign and date the masterpieces. Then take them to the local office supply or stationery store and have them laminated so they can be easily wiped clean.

22 Sweet Treat Tradition

Have each family member decorate the margins of a large recipe card using old greeting cards, markers, and craft supplies. Add delicious dessert recipes, then laminate the cards. You may want to give your children these recipe cards when they get married or to celebrate the birth of a child.

23 Raise the Family Flag

Celebrate being a family by raising a flag. Start with a white banner (or pillowcase) and decorate it with fabric and fabric paint, using images that symbolize your family: hearts for love, hands for helping, a music note for musicians, a wrapped gift for generosity, or a teddy bear for families that hug. Declare an official "Family Day," and begin it with a flag-raising ceremony.

24 We Belong Together

Create a family shirt to wear on special family outings. You'll need a white or light-colored T-shirt for each family member (prewashed), fabric paint, and sponges cut in various shapes. Decide as a family what your logo will be and use a sponge shape to stamp that logo onto your shirt. Place cardboard inside the shirt. Dip the sponge into the paint, blot it on a paper towel, then press it evenly onto the front of the shirt. Using black paint, print above the logo: "We Belong Together." Under the logo print your family name. Let the paint dry as directed on the bottle.

25 Flannel Fun

Bring your favorite stories to life with an old-fashioned flannel story board. Have your children help you cover a piece of sturdy cardboard with plain flannel fabric. Then create characters from pieces of colorful felt or glue magazine and coloring-book figures to the smooth side of a sheet of sandpaper and cut them out.

26 "Stained-Glass" Crayons

Gather all your broken, discarded crayons (the more colors the better!). Preheat oven to 300°. Line a loaf pan with tin foil, and add a 1-inch layer of crayon pieces (wrappers removed). Place in oven. Remove when crayons are shiny and beginning to melt (about 5 minutes). Cool until solid but warm, then cut into crayon shapes. Surprise Dad with a colorful "Welcome Home" banner made from white butcher paper and decorated with the stained-glass crayons.

27 Tell It on the Mountain!

Get your children in on the fun of a family newsletter! For a homey feel, use candid photos of your daily life. Include articles that show your family's heart. Older children can review favorite books and report on recitals and games they've attended. A little one can draw a picture of the family pet. The baby can contribute a handprint. Photocopy and send the newsletter to family and friends, but keep the original for your scrapbook!

28 New Year Wishes

Keep a journal of your New Year's Wishes. Mom and Dad, do you wish for a weekend getaway? Does Junior wish he could go fishing with Dad once a month? Do you want to find a family hobby? Talk about ways to make your wishes come true. Bring out your journal of Family Wishes each year and read through them. Add comments about your experiences and note those wishes that came true. Encourage your family to pursue their dreams!

We can make our plans, but the LORD determines our steps.
THE BOOK OF PROVERBS

2:9: What's for Dinner?

Answer the "What's for dinner?" question easily by making a chalkboard menu. Decorate the top of a medium-size chalkboard with greenery or silk flowers and a bow. Write out your menu, then place the chalkboard on an easel on your countertop.

30 Creative Countdown

Create a photo countdown to a birthday or other special event. Start at least two weeks before the anticipated occasion and brainstorm photo ideas: Day one, 1 cute teddy bear; Day two, 2 kids dressed in red; Day three, 3 kids hanging upside down from monkey bars; and so on. Have the pictures developed. Lay the photos out, then glue them onto a large sheet of poster board. Lay a second sheet of poster board over the first, and cut doors for each photo. Glue the two poster boards together. Print the number of the day on the outside of each door, and tape the doors closed. Add a title like "PJ's Birthday Countdown" across the top. Decorate with stickers, buttons, bows, and so on. Punch two holes at the top of the calendar and hang it with a sturdy cord. Every morning open a door—and watch as the excitement and anticipation builds in your children!

31 Mom's Survival Kit

For long car rides or everyday shopping trips, Mom's Survival Kit is indispensable. Select a basket that fits easily in your car and line it with a colorful piece of fabric. Fill the basket with things that interest your children: a coloring book and a new box of crayons, books to read, small toys, a cassette player with headphones and tapes. And don't forget food for hungry tummies: snack bars, boxes of juice or bottled water, and other goodies. Other essentials: tissues (for sniffles), premoistened towelettes, and a small first-aid kit.

32 Our Art Gallery

Create a wall-friendly children's gallery for hanging and rearranging art. Supplies: narrow rope or cord; 2 red wooden hearts; and wooden clothespins (for hanging the art).

Measure a length of rope long enough to span your art gallery wall and then add another three feet to that measurement. Tie a slipknot on each end of the rope for securing the line to the wall. Hot glue a cheery red heart to the slipknot and either fray or knot the "tail" left on the ends. Then have your children paint colorful clothespins to hang their artwork with.

33 Cheer for Students

Surprise your older children with an after-school craft party. Have the table set with supplies and craft ideas. Also make sure you provide lots of brain food to power their creative thinking, foods like warm, buttery popcorn, creamy fudge, or ice cream sundaes.

34 Basket of Blessings

When you give someone a blessing you are passing on the gift of hope and love. One well-known blessing from the Bible reads:

May the LORD bless you and protect you. May the LORD smile on you and be gracious to you. May the LORD show you his favor and give you his peace.
—THE BOOK OF NUMBERS

Think of simple, meaningful blessings you would like to pass on to your family and friends. Have your children help you to write them on small sheets of paper, roll them up, and tie them with ribbon. Place them in a pretty basket near the front door. When guests come to visit, invite them to take a blessing.

35 Cookie-Cutter Tablecloth

Create this one-of-a-kind tablecloth by gathering your family around the table for some cookie-cutter stamping! Lay out various cookie cutters. Spread a sheet on your table (with newspaper under it). Dip the cookie cutters into a puddle of fabric paint spread on a paper plate. Press the cookie cutters onto the sheet. Layer the designs, or repeat one or two motifs over and over again. Images may be left as is, colored with fabric markers, or accented with glitter and bows.

36 A "Homey" Hotel Vacation

Clear your schedule, turn your answering machine on, and imagine that your home is a fine hotel. Give your "hotel" a name and have the kids make up a sign to post on the front door. Stock your kitchen with food you love to order from room service. Then take turns being "the guest." (Family members should agree to promptly deliver room service when "the guest" rings a bell.)

37 Summer Memories Museum

On a shelf or curio cabinet, create a Summer Memories Museum that is filled with your family's most endearing summer treasures. During the summer have your children collect interesting rocks, shells, and flowers. Arrange their finds around family-at-play pictures, camp crafts, vacation souvenirs, and the summer book you read together. Feature your children's art and stories based on summer fun: watermelon feasts, chasing fireflies, watching fireworks, going on family picnics and bike rides. On frosty winter days, give your family a "tour" of your summer memories, admiring and talking about each item. The Summer Memories Museum will brighten your days all year long!

38 Relive Those Happy Days

Devote an evening to the fabulous fifties! Eat bologna sandwiches on white bread with mayonnaise and serve with red Jello, potato chips, and an ice-cold glass of Kool-Aid.

The Look: Men and boys—slicked-back hair, classic blue jeans, and white T-shirts. Women and girls—hair in ponytails, neck scarves, and poodle-shaped cutouts pinned to their skirts.

Play fifties games such as "Twister," or have a hula-hoop marathon. Watch classic black-and-white TV shows such as "I Love Lucy," "Father Knows Best," and "Andy Griffith."

39 Tour Your Own Hometown

Think about places a tourist would visit in your community. If you need a few ideas, check with your local Chamber of Commerce or contact the Automobile Club for historical points of interest and tourist spots in your area. Plan a day to play tourists!

4⊙ An Imaginary Trip Abroad

Take an imaginary trip to a country you'd like to visit. Make passports for family members. Have each person glue in his or her photo—or a magazine picture for a new identity. Note in your passport what you've discovered about "your" country: What language is spoken? What is it known for? What events happened there? What do they eat? What games do they play? Also list the cities and sights you'd like to see. Learn how to say a word or common phrase in the language of your country. Plan a menu that includes unusual dishes eaten there. Celebrate one of their national holidays.

41 Hungry Sock Monster Game

What's silly, brown, and loves to eat socks? A Sock Monster! They're wonderful pets and feeding them is great family fun.

In a grocery sack cut out a large circle for the monster's mouth. Next draw a funny face. Open the sack, fold the top down 1 inch, then staple it closed. Feeding your pet is simple. Roll up some socks. Each player stands a distance away and "feeds" the monster by tossing socks into his mouth. The one who gets the most socks into the hungry Sock Monster's mouth wins!

42 Backward Night

Plan a "Backward Night" where you do everything backwards. When the family arrives home for the evening, greet them with a kiss and wish them a "good night's sleep." Invite them to gather in the living room for a short bedtime story. Afterward, everyone brushes their teeth, takes a bath, and gets into their P.J.s. With teddy bears in hand, everyone heads to the dinner table for a yummy dessert! Don't forget to warn them: "If you don't eat your dessert, there will be no dinner!" Dessert is followed by a nourishing dinner, and . . . Well, you get the idea. You'll have an evening your children won't soon forget.

43 School-Day Picnic

Brighten up a humdrum school day with a surprise picnic. Your children will be thrilled when you arrive unannounced to treat them to a yummy picnic lunch and some extra special time with you. Take them to a picnic in the park or drive to a scenic location and have an impromptu picnic in your car. Bring a large blanket, festive napkins and plates, a vase with flowers, and their favorite foods.

44 Homework Holiday

Surprise your hard-working student with a homework holiday! Instead of doing homework in the usual place, head to the sandy shores of a sun-kissed beach or lake, or choose a quiet retreat under some shade trees at a local park. Later, after the homework is finished, take some time to play. Both you and your child will benefit when you begin to find creative ways to add simple pleasures to everyday life.

45 Long Distance Birthday

Strengthen your heart connection with family and friends who live far away by celebrating their birthdays long distance. Bake or buy a birthday cake in their honor, then call them to let them know you're celebrating their special day. Sing "Happy Birthday" and blow out the candles on their cake. Snap a photo of the long-distance event and send a copy with a cheerful handmade note that reads:

Your Birthday Is an Occasion Worth Celebrating! We Love You!

46 Mom's Hall of Fame

Place a bulletin board or chalkboard in a prominent place in your home and name it "Mom's Hall of Fame." Proudly post on it everyone's latest achievements—big or small. Make sure you include something for each family member and update it often. Your children will love to see their names in "Mom's Hall of Fame."

47 Kid Cafe

Treat the family to a meal at "Kid Cafe." Let your children play the parts of a cook and restauranteur. You play the part of a hungry customer. First, your children should make a list of foods they can make without your help: peanut butter and jelly sandwiches, baked potatoes, soup, macaroni and cheese, scrambled eggs, fruit salad, pudding. After they create an official menu, Kid Cafe is ready for business!

With aprons, paper pads, and pencils they're ready to take your order! (They may need to take the orders early.) Remember to compliment the chef and the waiter. Tip generously for good service and a kitchen that's left clean and tidy.

48 Your Children Are Stars!

Your children can star in their own "how to" video, demonstrating their skills: cooking, making paper airplanes, pitching a baseball, and so on. They should plan 5- to 10-minute presentations. They also need to select costumes, gather the props they need, and rehearse. Then, in their own way, they act out and explain each step of their skill.

49 Toy Story

Help your child create a storybook! First, choose a well-known tale or make up your own. Your children's toys will be the actors, so assign each one a role. Use things you have on hand for props. Look for indoor and outdoor locations for "sets." Take the toys through each scene, placing them in different positions with different props. Snap a picture each time you change a scene.

Develop the film, arrange the photos in order, and place them in a photo album next to colorfully decorated 3x5 cards on which you or the child has written lines from the story.

50 "I Remember You!"

This game uses pictures of family and friends! Mount 20 photos of familiar people on white paper. Make three copies (on card stock, laminate if possible), then cut the copies into identical shapes to make a "deck" of playing cards.

Goal: Collect three matching cards. *Play:* Deal four cards, face down, to each player. Take turns asking for a card that matches one you have: "Do you have a picture of someone in blue shoes?" If the other player has a match, it is handed over. If not, the "asker" draws from the deck (if there are no extra cards, asker draws from another player). The player with three matching cards shouts: "I Remember You!" then talks about the people or occasion in the picture.

51 Rainy Day Garden

Collect some rainwater in a jar. Cut off the lid of an egg carton. Fill the "cups" in the bottom of the carton with soil. Plant a flower seed in each one; water gently. Glue the seed packet to a stick and place it in the dirt. Talk about what would happen if it never rained. Then put the carton in a window, watering it with spoonfuls of rainwater each day.

52 Rainy Day Fun

Don't let a rainy day spoil your fun! Start a rainy-day journal. Jot down things you'd like to do on a rainy day. Bring it out whenever the sky turns gray.

53 Safe at Night with My Love

To make dark nights less scary, fill them with the light of your love. Turn a flashlight face down on black construction paper. Trace around the edge, then cut out the circle. Fold it in half, and cut a small heart out of the center. Open it up and tape the circle to the flashlight. At night, tuck your children in bed with blessings and hugs. Then place the flashlight conveniently by their sides. Tell them to shine the flashlight on the wall if they get scared. Let them know that the heart shining on their wall is a reminder that your heart is with them even when it's dark.

54. Message of Love

Inflate a balloon, write a loving message on it with a permanent marker, then deflate it. Tuck it into a lunch box, coat pocket, or purse to brighten your loved one's day.

55 Personal Bulletin Boards

Bulletin boards are an easy way to offer older children some space to call their own. Mount the bulletin boards in a convenient location in their room. Let them decorate using craft supplies and fabrics. Provide push pins. Encourage them to use the boards to post reminders, schoolwork, cartoons, artwork, and so on. Give them scrapbooks to save the outdated items, so they will feel free to update their bulletin boards often.

5.6 My Favorite Things Collage

Gather old magazines and let the children cut out interesting pictures. Separate them into categories: animals, plants, cars, clothes, food, people, toys, hobbies, sports, and so on. Have the children write "My Favorite Things" across the top of a piece of colored construction paper, then glue a photo of themselves in the middle of the page. Next they select a favorite picture from each category. After they arrange them into a collage around the photo, they can add any comments or explanations. Make sure they sign and date their works of art.

57 A Heart in a Hand

A hand-shape with a heart in the middle symbolizes "a helping hand filled with love." Whip up a batch of your favorite gingerbread. Trace your child's hand on poster board for a template to create hand-shape cookies. Then cut out small heart shapes to create the "love spot" in the palm. Let your child experience giving with a cheerful heart by hand-delivering these loving sweets to someone he cherishes.

58 A Story of Love

Have your child make a book filled with words of love, admiration, and colorful illustrations for a grandma or grandpa. The experience of writing a story about someone your child loves will reaffirm the importance of what is most precious in life—the people we hold dear to our hearts. Be sure the book is signed and dated. Adding a photo of the author would also be a sweet and memorable touch.

59 A "Garden" Party

The next time you're hauling in new soil for the garden, don't waste it on just the tomatoes. Plan a family dirt party and enjoy the good earth together before you plant the garden! Pile the dirt in a big mountain in the middle of the garden plot, scatter an assortment of beach toys and plastic shovels. Buy a big, juicy watermelon for refreshment.

Life in the Clouds

When it's time for the kids to take a nap or rest (and you need a break too!), take blankets and pillows out to the front yard or back deck. Have everybody lie down on their backs and look up. Then find cloud formations that look like real-life objects: flowers, dolphins, hammers—even Grandma! The person who "sees" something describes it so the others can see it too.

Summer Water Olympics

In the heat of the summer, host "The Water Olympics" in your own yard! Create an obstacle course. Gather and set up (waterproof) items to crawl over and under, run around, and walk through. Use a hose or sprinkler for the "water hazard." You can also set up relays, ball tosses, and other games. Invite other kids to ensure plenty of participants.

6.2 The Spirit of Giving

Help your children discover the delight of giving without expecting anything in return. Each week have *everyone* in the family put aside some of their spending money to create a special gift fund. Next, the whole family looks for people (friends or strangers) who need something or could use encouragement. As a family, decide who the recipient will be and what the present will be (if the gift is cash, make a card together—but don't sign it!). Secretly deliver the gift to the recipient.

6.3 Sharing Family Memories

Gather the family in a circle and place the pictures that never got sorted and put away in the center. Give everyone a small photo album or scrapbook page, and have them put together their own "family album." Talk about the people and events shown in the pictures. This is a great time to pass on family history, memories, and stories to the next generation, and you'll get your pictures sorted and put away!

6.4 A Box of Love

If a special person or family member can't make it home for the holidays, send her a box of love. Set a box labeled with the person's name in a prominent place a few weeks before the festivities. Have everyone in the family contribute items to the box, include notes telling the loved one how much she is loved and missed.

6.5 A Special Date

A perfect way to discover the interests and activities of your children is to take each one of them on a "date." This one-on-one time with Mom or Dad will create a lasting memory and strengthen the bond between you and your child.

The date can be simple or fancy. Choose an activity you both enjoy that allows time to interact and talk. Bring your camera and have someone take a photo of the two of you. Frame one for yourself and one for your special date.

66. Birthday Traditions

Start a birthday tradition by giving roses or collectibles (baseball cards, interesting rocks, unusual coins)—one for each year. Let the birthday child skip doing chores on the special day. Have a "You're Special" plate that only the birthday person can use. Let the birthday person choose the menu for dinner that evening.

67. Pajama Ride!

After you have just tucked your kids into bed, burst into their room and yell, "Pajama Ride!" Put their coats on, get in the car, and go out for ice cream cones. The kids will remember this surprise forever.

6.8 Just You and Me

Invite your child to join you on a special pre-birthday date each year. Take her to her favorite restaurant or dessert spot. Share with her how excited you are about how she is growing up. Talk about the changes you have noticed in her, such as learning new skills, accepting more responsibility. Ask her about her own goals and desires for the next year, and by all means reaffirm your unconditional love for her. You'll be creating a birthday tradition your child will look forward to year after year.

6.9 Create Your Own Holiday

When your child needs encouragement or a break, declare a "Jolly Day"—a special time of celebration. Let your child select something special to do: go out for ice cream, play a favorite game, stay up a half hour past bedtime. Make the activity extra-special with treats, a small gift, and private time with you.

70 Room Service

On a regular, everyday sort of evening, surprise your children just before bedtime with trays of milk and cookies. Sit and talk about their day, their dreams, their goals. Before the lights go out, have them reach under their pillows for the small tokens of affection you have previously hidden.

71 Breakfast Sundaes

Put some sparkle into your morning routine by offering these great-tasting (and nutritous) breakfast sundaes. Provide containers of vanilla and/or fruit-flavored yogurt, fresh or canned fruit, nuts, granola, and even some colored cake sprinkles. Let your children create their own sundaes.

72 Celebrating in Style

Most children look forward to planning a costume for harvest celebrations, but costumes can brighten up other holidays too! Encourage your children to come to Thanksgiving dinner disguised as Indians or dress up as their favorite president on Presidents' Day. Perhaps you can have a day to dress up as favorite occupations—fireman, teacher, doctor, and so on. Or let the kids satisfy their creative cravings by having a neighborhood "dress-up" day, complete with a parade to show off the costumes.

73 A Half-Birthday

For a special treat, have a "half-birthday" six months after your child's last birthday. Carry out the half theme by serving half a birthday cake, half portions of ice cream and soda, and so on. Tell guests the only gift required is a smile and a willingness to have a good time.

74 Saturday Traditions

Saturday is probably the most flexible day of the week for creating family memories. Make some of these family activities your own traditions to be passed from generation to generation:

- picnics in the park
- flying kites
- visiting Grandma
- backyard barbecues
- traditional pancake breakfast that Dad cooks
- roasting marshmallows in the fireplace

75 Miniature Bouquets

Take your children into your garden (or arrange to visit someone else's garden) and show them how to pick miniature bouquets. Gather miniature roses, violets, and honeysuckle. Tie slender ribbons around the little nosegays and pop them into pill bottles or miniature vases. Display these little bouquets next to dinner plates, on mantels, or on windowsills.

76 The Time Capsule

Start with a box that you have decorated. Fill the box with some of these items: a current newspaper and magazine, pictures and a video of you and your family, a favorite toy or baseball card, a tape recording of your voice, lists of your favorite movies, ice cream flavors, games, sports, and so on. Include short paragraphs written by each family member about the best and worst thing that happened this year. Decide where you want to hide your time capsule and when you will open it—1 year? 5 years? 10 years? Then stash the box until it's time to rediscover the thoughts and memories of "way back then"!

77 A Kid's Fort

Let your kids do this activity on their own! Choose the ideal spot—indoors or outdoors, depending on the weather. Then give your kids everything they'll need to create the perfect fort: a card table, old sheets and blankets, a stepladder, rope, etc. Include fun things to have inside the fort: a flashlight, stuffed animals, pots and pans, old clothes, and jewelry. Serve special fort snacks to your creative engineers.

78 Grandparents' Journal

Your children can get to know their grandparents by sending them a question about their lives. Ask Grandpa and Grandma to write back or tape record the answer. Do this once a week, and soon you will have a wonderful journal of their memories!

79 Teddy Bear Pancake Party

Surprise the teddy bear lover in your family with this festive party. Decorate the center of your table with teddy bears—place them in a basket tied with a big bow or in a small toy wagon filled with hay. Make teddy bear-shaped place cards and give everyone a bear name (Mama bear, Baby bear).

Then whip up your favorite pancake recipe. With a serving spoon, slowly drizzle the batter on a hot griddle to form two small ears (an inch apart), then add a large dollop for the face. Serve with maple syrup, fresh berries, and happy music!

80 ★ A Barnyard Peanut Hunt

This barn game can be played any-where! Hide shelled peanuts all over the house. Have your children invite a few friends over. Divide into teams (three or more people per team). Hand out paper bags—one per team. Each group should choose a leader and the name of a barn-yard animal (chicken, cow, and so on).

Set a timer for 15 minutes. The leader holds the bag and is the *only* person allowed to pick up the team's peanuts. The rest of the team searches for the peanuts. When someone finds a peanut, he or she makes the sound of the team's animal. The team leader, upon hearing the sound, runs over and puts the peanut in the bag. The team who gathers the most peanuts wins.

81 A Blessing Tree

Find some pretty paper and cut several shapes for each season. Have each person write what he or she is thankful for on the back of one of the shapes. Next, get a bare tree branch, put it into a flowerpot, and secure it with rocks or plaster of paris. Punch a hole at the top of each season shape, insert a ribbon, and tie it to your Blessing Tree. Review and update these blessings often.

82 Family Story Time

Recapture the joy of this old-fashioned pastime, and get the whole family involved. Pick a favorite book, then every evening read a whole chapter aloud. Make things interesting by taking turns reading, or assign parts and read the stories like a play.

83 Paper Chain Fun

Create a paper chain to measure your family's accomplishments. Begin by cutting colorful paper into same-length strips. On the paper strips, record the goals members of your family complete: a difficult homework assignment, the completion of a work project, practiced piano every day for 30 minutes, lost five pounds, etc. Then add the links to your chain by pasting the ends of the strips together. Every time your family looks at the chain, they'll be reminded of everything they've successfully accomplished!

84 Family Drama

Collect a box full of old hats, shirts, trousers, dresses, costume jewelry, eyeglasses, scarves, and anything else that would make for a good costume. With a little creativity and imagination, put on a play dealing with topics such as: kindness, honesty, courage, compassion, thankfulness, and love. Keep the video camera ready to record this very special family production.

85 Family-Room Camp Out

Bring out your sleeping bags and pillows and set up your campsite on the family-room floor in front of the fireplace (or use a candle in a jar as your campfire). Turn out the lights, then sing old campfire songs, tell funny stories, and see who can make the silliest face while shining a flashlight under their chin.

86 The Nose Knows

This is a fun game for a rainy afternoon. Prepare a tray of several foods in separate paper cups: a slice of lemon, slices of banana, a dab of mustard, garlic, taco sauce, green olives, apple slices, soda, a potato chip, piece of bread, cookie dough, and anything else you have on hand. Conceal the contents so your children can't see what's in the cups. Blindfold each child and let him or her smell each food and guess what it is.

87 Story-Go-Round

At the dinner table have one person make up a title to a story—then begin to tell the tale. Have that person say one or two lines, then the next person adds to it. Go around until everyone has contributed. The very last person gives the story a happy ending. Each time you create a new story, tape record it and take it along for hilarious entertainment on your next long car trip.

88 Please Write...

At least once a month, gather the family together for a "letter-writing festival"—where each family member writes to a friend or relative. Play classical music in the background and serve a special treat to eat to make this a happy event.

89 The Table of Treasures

On a warm Saturday morning, round up the family for a treasure hunt at a local swap meet, garage sale, or flea market. Your quest: Find little creamer pitchers and a dinner plate for each family member. Each person should find a dish that best reflects his personality. With a paint pen, write the person's name and date on the back of the plate, along with any other comments.

Then create a beautiful table, set with a variety of different plate designs, and little creamer "vases" adorned with tiny colorful flowers, each as unique as the person who graces that spot.

90 I Like That Southern Drawl!

Take turns reading a book aloud using different accents. Give that character voice a name: Savannah, the beautiful Southern Belle; Remington, the Englishman; Joe, the New Yorker; Tony, the Italian; Brittany, the valley girl! This will add drama, excitement, and a lot of humor to the reading hour. At each family reading session, request that one of the characters read aloud. (Will "Savannah" please read the next selection in her southern drawl?)

91 Dessert Anyone?

Pick a regular dessert time: Sunday afternoons, Tuesday nights, the last Friday of the month. Make it a tradition to always serve the family's favorite treats in the same dessert cups. Someday, those dessert cups will trigger nostalgic thought.

He...fed him with the fruit of the fields. He nourished him with honey. THE BOOK OF DEUTERONOMY

92 The Chin Family Follies

Host the Chin Family Puppet Show. Choose who will be members of the Chin Family and who will be the audience. With an eyebrow pencil, draw eyes and a nose on each person's chin—(the eyes on the bottom, the nose above the eyes). Apply red lipstick to each person's lips. The Chin Family will then lay on their backs on an ottoman or bench with their heads hanging down. Have each Chin Family member cover the rest of his or her face with a towel. Only the chin and mouth should show.

Now the fun begins. Have the Chin Family lip-synch to music or carry on a conversation with each other. The results are hilarious. Make sure you have the video camera ready!

93 The Good News Is . . .

Designate one day a week for each child to find a positive article in the newspaper or a magazine and share it with the family during dinnertime. Have your child give a short summary, then comment on the article. Encourage interaction by asking questions and discussing the news item.

94 Growing Gardeners

Growing a vegetable garden and selling the produce to Mom (at the same price or less than she would pay at the grocery store) helps kids fill the piggy bank and provides a great learning experience. Let the kids have fun mapping out the garden and getting planting ideas from seed catalogs. Help them understand what the daily responsibilities of a garden are: planting, watering, fertilizing, weeding, and harvesting. Then let them take over. A garden will teach them that "we reap what we sow."

95 Ready, Set, Go!

Get ready early for spur-of-the-moment summertime picnics!
Wash out the cooler, and let your children help you pack your picnic basket with:

- bottle/can opener
- sharp knife
- paper towels
- matches
- plates, cups, flatware
- picnic blanket and tablecloth
- salt and pepper shakers

- napkins
- first aid kit
- trash bags
- camera and extra film
- sunscreen
- hand soap
- sunglasses and hats

You'll be prepared to go on a picnic at the drop of a hat!

Money Matters

A simple way to teach your child to be responsible with money is to supply him with three jars labeled as follows:

1. Save—for the future
2. Spend—for enjoyment
3. Share—with church or charity

Explain the importance of handling money, and discuss saving, spending, and sharing. Help your child budget a certain portion of his money for each category. Encourage him to follow-through. From time to time, take your child to the bank to deposit his savings in his own account. Guide him in his giving, and let him know how proud you are to see his willingness to share.

97 Mama's Favorite Apron

Give your children a plain white apron and fabric paints. Let them decorate the apron with apple stamps: Cut an apple in half from stem to bottom. Paint the inside using red fabric paint and a paintbrush. Press the apple against the apron. With fabric paint, add a brown stem and a green leaf. Let the children paint their hands and make handprints on the apron. Also have them sign their names and write their ages under the handprints. Now take a black paint pen and write "(child's name) is the apple of my eye!" for each child. Let the apron dry. Wear this apron every time you cook as a reminder to them that you love them.

My Favorite Things

For a great inside activity, have your children decorate a "special treasures" box. Set out paints, glitter, colored markers, and other craft supplies. Explain that the box they are making will be the perfect place to keep the wonderful things they collect: rocks, shells, marbles, photos, poems, artwork, letters, a piece of their blankie, favorite shoes, a special book, and so on. Every once in a while, get out the video camera and encourage your children to share with you the stories and memories behind the keepsakes stored in the "special treasures" box.

Pictures for Memories

For the next family event purchase a disposable camera for each person in the family. With just a few instructions on how to operate the camera, including keeping still when the snapshot button is pushed, children can capture their own photo memories. When the pictures are developed, family members can create their own scrapbook pages to preserve those special moments in time.

Tip: To keep the cameras and film from getting mixed up, write the person's name on the camera and immediately take a picture of the camera's owner. This way, when the developed pictures are picked up, the first photo will show the owner.

100 ✿✿ Famous Actions

Everyone should be known for something they do well. Mom may be famous for her spaghetti sauce, Grandpa may be known for always whistling a happy tune, and Sister for having a bright cheerful smile. Make it a habit to point out the good things your family members are "famous" for. "I sure could use one of Dad's famous bear hugs right about now!" will brighten up the day for Dad and the person requesting the hug.

101 Table Talk

To help start conversations at mealtime, have each person take turns answering the "Question of the Day":

• What do you love most about each person in our family?

• What is your favorite joke?

• Describe the perfect day.

• What was your favorite part of the day today?

May the words of my mouth and the thoughts of my heart be pleasing to you, O Lord...
THE BOOK OF PSALMS